The Black Cat
and Other Stories

EDGAR ALLAN POE

Level 3

Retold by David Wharry
Series Editors: Andy Hopkins and Jocelyn Potter

Pearson Education Limited
Edinburgh Gate, Harlow,
Essex CM20 2JE, England
and Associated Companies throughout the world.

ISBN: 978-1-4058-7662-9

This adaptation first published by Penguin Books Ltd 1991
Published by Addison Wesley Longman Ltd and Penguin Books Ltd 1998
New edition first published 1999
This edition first published 2008

10

Text copyright © David Wharry 1991
Illustrations copyright © David Cuzik 1991

Typeset by Graphicraft Ltd, Hong Kong
Set in 11/14pt Bembo
Printed in China
SWTC/10

Published by Pearson Education Ltd

Every effort has been made to trace the copyright holders and we apologise in advance for any
unintentional omissions. We would be pleased to insert the appropriate acknowledgement in any
subsequent edition of this publication.

For a complete list of the titles available in the Pearson English Readers series, please
visit www.pearsonenglishreaders.com. Alternatively, write to your local Pearson Education
office or to Pearson English Readers Marketing Department, Pearson Education,
Edinburgh Gate, Harlow, Essex CM20 2JE, England.

Contents

Contents

Introduction

Slowly, this strange fear grew into horror. Yes, horror. If I tell you why, you will not believe me. You will think I am mad.

The *Black Cat* is one of Edgar Allan Poe's most famous horror stories. Why is the man in the story afraid of his own black cat? Why does he kill it? And how does the cat punish him for his evil ways?

In *The Oval Portrait* a man finds a portrait of a beautiful young woman in a lonely house. Who is this woman? Who painted her? And why is the man so frightened of her picture? What terrible secret does it hold?

In *Berenice*, a madman offers to marry his sick cousin. He does not love her but she loves him. One day after she smiles at him, he cannot stop thinking about her beautiful teeth. What really happens to Berenice in the end?

In *The Mask of the Red Death*, a terrible illness is killing people in the city. Prince Prospero takes a thousand friends away from the city and tries to shut his door against the face of Death. How does the 'Red Death' get into his large house? What will happen to him and all his friends when they meet the stranger with the red mask of death?

Here, you will read four horror stories from the strange and terrible mind of Edgar Allan Poe. They are stories about beauty, evil and death. Will they stop you sleeping at night?

No writer knew more about pain and horror than Edgar Allan Poe. He lived most of his life afraid of the things in his own mind. And he wrote some of the most frightening horror stories ever written.

He was born Edgar Poe on 19 January 1809 in Boston,

Massachusetts in the United States. When he was two years old, his mother died. His father died or left the family (Nobody knows exactly what happened to him). So young Edgar Poe went to live with a family called Allan in Richmond, Virginia. At this time, he added their surname to his. The Allans were a rich family, and Mrs Allan loved him like a real son. But her husband, Mr Allan, never understood Poe and he was unkind to the boy. The family moved to England for five years from 1815, and Poe went to one of the best schools in the country. In 1820 he returned to Virginia and went to university there in 1826. When he was a student there his life started to go badly wrong. John Allan refused to pay for his university because the boy was spending too much money. This hurt Poe very deeply. The dislike between him and John Allan grew, and in 1827 he left the Allans' home for ever.

Poe became a successful soldier for a few years. Then he went to Baltimore, Maryland, and earned money by writing for newspapers and magazines. He also worked on a magazine in Richmond, Virginia, but he didn't go back to his old home.

When Poe was twenty-six, in 1835, he married his young cousin, Virginia Clemm. She was much younger than him, and their married life together was difficult. Poe worked hard but he didn't earn much money. He never stayed long in one job. He was a nervous man, and he drank too much all his life. He also believed that he was mad.

In 1847, Virginia died after a long illness. Poe's home life ended and he began to drink more than before. Then, his luck changed. In 1849 Poe met a friend from his school days – she was now called Mrs Shelton. When they were children, he liked her very much. Her husband was dead, so Poe asked her to marry him. She accepted and they happily planned their wedding. He was forty years old, and he thought that his troubles were finished at last. But in September of that year, he suddenly disappeared. Nobody knows why. He was later found lying in a street in Baltimore. He was taken to hospital, where he died on 7 October 1849. He was buried in Baltimore, next to his wife.

Poe was very unhappy for much of his life, and when he died he was still a poor man. He earned only about fifteen dollars for each of his stories. But by the end of his life he was beginning to be a very popular and successful writer. Many people, first in France and later in America, were reading and enjoying his stories and poems.

His poem *The Raven* (1845) is a cry for lost love and is one of the best-known poems in American literature. Since his death, Poe has become one of the most famous of all American writers. His stories and poems are now read by people all over the world.

Poe's horror stories, like the four in this book, are very cleverly written, full of imagination. People read them in American magazines from 1831, and in books called *Tales of the Grotesque and Arabesque* (1840) and *Tales* (1845). Some of his most famous stories are in this Pearson English Reader. Other famous stories are 'The Fall of the House of Usher' (1839), 'The Murders in the Rue Morgue' (1841), and 'The Pit and the Pendulum' (1843).

Poe had a strange imagination and one of the saddest lives in all of literature. His terrible stories touch our deepest fears and are difficult to forget.

*This is a true story, as true as I sit here writing it – as true as
I will die in the morning.*

The Black Cat

You are not going to believe this story. But it is a true story, as true as I sit here writing it – as true as I will die in the morning. Yes, this story ends with *my* end, with my death tomorrow.

I have always been a kind and loving person – everyone will tell you this. They will also tell you that I have always loved animals more than anything. When I was a little boy, my family always had many different animals round the house. As I grew up, I spent most of my time with them, giving them their food and cleaning them.

I married when I was very young, and I was happy to find that my wife loved all of our animal friends as much as I did. She bought us the most beautiful animals. We had all sorts of birds, gold fish, a fine dog and *a cat*.

The cat was a very large and beautiful animal. He was black, black all over, and *very* intelligent. He was so intelligent that my wife often laughed about what some people believe; some people believe that all black cats are evil, enemies in a cat's body.

Pluto – this was the cat's name – was my favourite. It was always I who gave him his food, and he followed me everywhere. I often had to stop him from following me through the streets! For years, he and I lived happily together, the best of friends.

But during those years I was slowly changing. It was that evil enemy of Man called *Drink* who was changing me. I was not the kind, loving person people knew before. I grew more and more selfish. I was often suddenly angry about unimportant things. I began to use bad language, most of all with my

*I hit my wife sometimes. And by that time, of course, I was often
doing horrible things to our animals.*

wife. I even hit her sometimes. And by that time, of course, I
was often doing horrible things to our animals. I hit all of
them – but never Pluto. But, my illness was getting worse – oh
yes, drink is an illness! Soon I began to hurt my dear Pluto
too.

I remember that night very well. I came home late, full of
drink again. I could not understand why Pluto was not pleased
to see me. The cat was staying away from me. My Pluto did
not want to come near me! I caught him and picked him
up, holding him strongly. He was afraid of me and bit my
hand.

Suddenly, I was not myself any more. Someone else was in my

body: someone evil, and mad with drink! I took my knife from my pocket, held the poor animal by his neck and cut out one of his eyes.

The next morning, my mind was full of pain and horror when I woke up. I was deeply sorry. I could not understand how I could do such an evil thing. But drink soon helped me to forget.

Slowly the cat got better. Soon he felt no more pain. There was now only an ugly dry hole where the eye once was. He began to go round the house as usual again. He never came near me now, of course, and he ran away when I went too close.

I knew he didn't love me any more. At first I was sad. Then, slowly, I started to feel angry, and I did another terrible thing...

I had to do it – I could not stop myself. I did it with a terrible sadness in my heart – because I knew it was evil. And that was *why* I did it – yes! I did it *because I knew it was evil.* What did I do? I caught the cat and hung him by his neck from a tree until he was dead.

That night I woke up suddenly – my bed was on fire. I heard people outside shouting, 'Fire! Fire!' Our house was burning! I, my wife and our servant were lucky to escape. We stood and watched as the house burned down to the ground.

There was nothing left of the building the next morning. All the walls fell down during the night, except one – a wall in the middle of the house. I realized why this wall did not burn: because there was new plaster on it. The plaster was still quite wet.

I was surprised to see a crowd of people next to the wall. They were talking, and seemed to be quite excited. I went closer and looked over their shoulders. I saw a black shape in

3

I saw a black shape in the new white plaster. It was the shape of a large cat, hanging by its neck.

the new white plaster. It was the shape of a large cat, hanging by its neck.

I looked at the shape with complete horror. Several minutes passed before I could think clearly again. I knew I had to try to think clearly. I had to know why it was there.

I remembered hanging the cat in the garden of the house next door. During the fire the garden was full of people. Probably, someone cut the dead cat from the tree and threw it through the window – to try and wake me. The falling walls pressed the animal's body into the fresh plaster. The cat burned completely, leaving the black shape in the new plaster. Yes, I was sure that was what happened.

But I could not forget that black shape for months. I even saw it in my dreams. I began to feel sad about losing the animal. So I began to look for another one. I looked mostly in the poor parts of our town where I went drinking. I searched for another black cat, of the same size and type as Pluto.

One night, as I sat in a dark and dirty drinking-house, I noticed a black object on top of a cupboard, near some bottles of wine. I was surprised when I saw it. 'I looked at those bottles a few minutes ago,' I thought, 'and I am sure that object was not there before . . .'

I got up, and went to see what it was. I put my hand up, touched it, and found that it was a black cat – a very large one, as large as Pluto. He looked like Pluto too – in every way but one: Pluto did not have a white hair anywhere on his body; this cat had a large white shape on his front.

He got up when I touched him, and pressed the side of his head against my hand several times. He liked me. This was the animal I was looking for! He continued to be very friendly and later, when I left, he followed me into the street. He came all the way home with me – we now had another house – and came

5

inside. He immediately jumped up on to the most comfortable chair and went to sleep. He stayed with us, of course. He loved both of us and very soon he became my wife's favourite animal.

But, as the weeks passed, I began to dislike the animal more and more. I do not know why, but I hated the way he loved me. Soon, I began to hate him – but I was never unkind to him. Yes, I was very careful about that. I kept away from him because I remembered what I did to my poor Pluto. I also hated the animal because he only had one eye. I noticed this the morning after he came home with me. Of course, this only made my dear wife love him more!

But the more I hated the cat, the more he seemed to love me. He followed me everywhere, getting under my feet all the time. When I sat down, he always sat under my chair. Often he tried to jump up on my knees. I wanted to murder him when he did this, but I did not. I stopped myself because I remembered Pluto, but also because I was *afraid* of the animal.

How can I explain this fear? It was not really a fear of something evil...but then how else can I possibly describe it? Slowly, this strange fear grew into horror. Yes, *horror*. If I tell you why, you will not believe me. You will think I am mad.

Several times, my wife took the cat and showed me the white shape on his chest. She said the shape was slowly changing. For a long time I did not believe her, but slowly, after many weeks, I began to see that she was right. The shape *was* changing. Its sides were becoming straighter and straighter. It was beginning to look more and more like an object...After a few more weeks, I saw what the shape was. It was impossible not to see! There, on his front, was the shape of an object I am almost too afraid to name...It

There, on the cat's front was the shape of that terrible machine of pain and death – the gallows!

was that terrible machine of pain and death – yes, the GALLOWS!*

I no longer knew the meaning of happiness, or rest. During the day, the animal never left me. At night he woke me up nearly every hour. I remember waking from terrible dreams and feeling him sitting next to my face, his heavy body pressing down on my *heart*!

I was now a very different man. There was not the smallest piece of good left in me. I now had only evil thoughts – the darkest and the most evil thoughts. I hated everyone and everything, my dear wife too.

One day she came down into the cellar with me to cut some wood (we were now too poor to have a servant). Of course, the

* *Gallows.* The place where criminals are hanged.

*I tried to cut the animal in two. My wife stopped my arm with
her hand. This made me even more angry.*

cat followed me down the stairs and nearly made me fall. This made me so angry, that I took the axe and tried to cut the animal in two. But as I brought the axe down, my wife stopped my arm with her hand. This made me even more angry, and I pulled her hand away from my wrist, lifted the tool again, brought it down hard and buried it in the top of her head.

I had to hide the body. I knew I could not take it out of the house. The neighbours noticed everything. I thought of cutting it into pieces and burning it. I thought of burying it in the floor of the cellar. I thought of throwing it into the river at the end of the garden. I thought of putting it into a wooden box and taking it out of the house that way. In the end, I decided to hide the body in one of the walls of the cellar.

It was quite an old building, near the river, so the walls of the cellar were quite wet and the plaster was soft. There was new plaster on one of the walls, and I knew that underneath it the wall was not very strong. I also knew that this wall was very thick. I could hide the body in the middle of it.

It was not difficult. I took off some plaster, took out a few stones and made a hole in the earth that filled the middle of the wall. I put my wife there, put back the stones, made some new plaster and put it on the wall. Then I cleaned the floor, and looked carefully round. Everything looked just as it did before. Nobody would ever know.

Next, I went upstairs to kill the cat. The animal was bringing me bad luck. I had to kill it. I searched everywhere, but I could not find him. I was sure it was because of my wife's murder; he was too clever to come near me now.

I waited all evening, but I did not see the evil animal. He did not come back during the night either. And so, for the first time in a long time, I slept well. When I woke up the next morning, I was surprised to see that the cat still was not there. Two, three days passed, and there was *still* no cat. I cannot tell you how happy I began to feel. I felt so much better without the cat. Yes, it was *he* who brought me all my unhappiness. And now, without him, I began to feel like a free man again. It was wonderful – no more cat! Never again!

Several people came and asked about my wife, but I answered their questions easily. Then, on the fourth day, the police came. I was not worried when they searched the house. They asked me to come with them as they searched. They looked everywhere, several times. Then they went down into the cellar. I went down with them, of course. I was not a bit afraid. I walked calmly up and down, watching them search.

They found nothing, of course, and soon they were ready to go. I was so happy that I could not stop talking as they went up the stairs. I did not really know what I was saying. 'Good day to you all, dear sirs.' I said. 'Yes, this is a well-built old house, isn't it? Yes, a *very* well-built old house. These walls – are you going, gentlemen? – these walls are *strong*, aren't they?' I knocked hard on the part of the wall where my wife was.

A voice came from inside the wall, in answer to my knock. It was a cry, like a child's. Quickly, it grew into a long scream of pain and horror. I saw the policemen standing on the stairs with their mouths open. Suddenly, they all ran down in a great hurry and began breaking down the wall. It fell quickly, and there was my wife, standing inside. There she was, with dried blood all over her head, looking at them. And there was the cat, standing on her head, his red mouth wide open in a scream, and his one gold eye shining like fire. The clever animal! My wife was dead because of him, and now his evil voice was sending me to the gallows.

There she was with dried blood all over her head. And there was the cat, standing on her head.

We saw the dark shape of the roof above the forest. It was a sad and strangely beautiful house.

The Oval Portrait

We saw the dark shape of the roof above the forest. It was not far away, but travelling was difficult in that wild part of the mountains. We did not arrive until night was falling.

It was a sad and strangely beautiful house, many hundreds of years old. Pedro, my servant, broke in through a small door at the back and carried me carefully inside. I was so badly hurt that I would die if we stayed out all night.

'People were living here until a very short time ago,' Pedro said. 'They left in a hurry.'

He carried me through several tall, richly decorated rooms to a smaller room in a corner of the great house. He helped me to lie down on the bed. There were a lot of very fine modern pictures in this room. I looked at them for a while in the dying light. They were everywhere on the walls, all round me.

After dark, I could not sleep because of the pain. Also, I was so weak now that I was afraid that I was dying. So I asked Pedro to light the lamp beside the bed.

I began to look at the pictures on the walls, and as I did so I read a small book. I found this book on the bed next to me. It described all the pictures in the room, one by one, and told their stories.

I looked and read for a long time, and the hours passed quickly. Midnight came and went. My eyes became more and more tired, and soon I found it hard to read the words on the page. So I reached out – this was painful and difficult – and moved the lamp closer. Now, the lamp's light fell in a different part of the room, a part that was in deep shadow until then. I saw more pictures, and among them there was a portrait of a young woman. As soon as I saw it, I closed my eyes.

13

Keeping my eyes closed, I tried to understand why. Why did I suddenly close my eyes like that? Then I realized. I did it to give myself time. I needed time to think. Was I sure that I *really* saw what I thought I saw? Was I dreaming? No, I was suddenly very awake.

I waited until I was calm again; then I opened my eyes and looked a second time. No, there was no mistake. My eyes were seeing what they saw the first time, only seconds before.

The picture, as I said, was a portrait. It was oval in shape, and showed the head and shoulders of a young woman. It was the finest and the most beautiful painting that I have ever seen. And I know I never ever saw a woman as beautiful as her! But it was not her beauty that shook me so suddenly from my half-sleep. And it was not the beauty of the painter's work that excited me in such a strange way.

I stayed for perhaps an hour, half-sitting, half-lying, never taking my eyes off the portrait. Then at last, I understood. At last, I realized what the *true* secret of the picture was, and I fell back in the bed again.

It was the way she was looking at me.

Her eyes, that beautiful smile, that way she looked at me – she was so *real*! It was almost impossible to believe that she was just paint – that she was not *alive*!

The first time I looked at the portrait I simply *could not believe* what my eyes were seeing. But now I felt a very different feeling growing inside me. The more I looked into those eyes, the more I looked at that beautiful smile, the more I was *afraid*! It was a strange, terrible fear that I could not understand. It was a fear mixed with horror.

I moved the lamp back to where it was before. The portrait was now hidden in darkness again. Quickly, I looked through the book until I found the story of the oval portrait. I read these words:

14

The picture was a portrait. It was oval in shape, and showed the head and shoulders of a young woman.

'She was a beautiful young flower, and always so happy. Yes, she was happy until that evil day when she saw and loved the painter of her portrait. They were married. But, sadly, he already had a wife: his work. His painting was more important to him than anything in the world.

'Before, she was all light and smiles. She loved everything in the world. Now she loved all things but one: her husband's work. His painting was her only enemy; and she began to hate the paintings that kept her husband away from her. And so it was a terrible thing when he told her that he wanted to paint his young wife's portrait.

'For weeks, she sat in the tall, dark room while he worked. He was a silent man, always working, always lost in his wild, secret dreams. She sat still – always smiling, never moving – while he painted her hour after hour, day after day. He did not see that she was growing weaker with every day. He never noticed that she was not healthy any more, and not happy any more. The change was happening in front of his eyes, but he did not see it.

'But she went on smiling. She never stopped smiling because she saw that her husband (who was now very famous) enjoyed his work so much. He worked day and night, painting the portrait of the woman he loved. And as he painted, the woman who loved him grew slowly weaker and sadder.

'Several people saw the half-finished picture. They told the painter how wonderful it was, speaking softly as he worked. They said the portrait showed how much he loved his beautiful wife. Silently, she sat in front of her husband and his visitors, hearing and seeing nothing now.

'The work was coming near an end. He did not welcome visitors in the room any more. A terrible fire was burning inside him now. He was wild, almost mad with his work. His eyes almost never left the painting now, even to look at his wife's face. Her face was as white as snow. The painter did not see that the colours he was painting were no longer there in her *real* face.

'Many more weeks passed until, one day, in the middle of winter, he finished the portrait. He touched the last paint on to her lips; he put the last, thin line of colour on an eye; then he stood back and looked at the finished work.

'As he looked, he began to shake. All colour left his face. With his eyes on the portrait, he cried out to the world: 'This woman is not made of paint! She is *alive*!' Then he turned suddenly to look at the woman he loved so much . . .

'She was dead.'

*Then he turned suddenly to look at the woman he loved
so much . . . She was dead.*

I almost never left the house, and I left the library less and less.

Berenice

Egaeus is my name. My family – I will not name it – is one of the oldest in the land. We have lived here, inside the walls of this great house, for many hundreds of years. I sometimes walk through its silent rooms. Each one is richly decorated, by the hands of only the finest workmen. But my favourite has always been the library. It is here, among books, that I have always spent most of my time.

My mother died in the library; I was born here. Yes, the world heard my first cries here; and these walls, the books that stand along them are among the first things I can remember in my life.

I was born here in this room, but my life did not begin here. I know I lived another life before the one I am living now. I can remember another time, like a dream without shape or body: a world of eyes, sweet sad sounds and silent shadows. I woke up from that long night, my eyes opened, and I saw the light of day again – here in this room full of thoughts and dreams.

As a child, I spent my days reading in this library, and my young days dreaming here. The years passed, I grew up without noticing it, and soon I found that I was no longer young. I was already in the middle of my life, and I was still living here in the house of my fathers.

I almost never left the house, and I left the library less and less. And so, slowly, the real world – life in the world outside these walls – began to seem like a dream to me. The wild ideas, the dreams *inside my head* were my real world. They were my whole life.

♦

Berenice and I were cousins. She and I grew up together here

19

in this house. But we grew so differently. I was the weak one, so often sick, always lost in my dark and heavy thoughts. She was the strong, healthy one, always so full of life, always shining like a bright new sun. She ran over the hills under the great blue sky while I studied in the library. I lived inside the walls of my mind, fighting with the most difficult and painful ideas. She walked quickly and happily through life, never thinking of the shadows around her. I watched our young years flying away on the silent wings of time. Berenice never thought of tomorrow. She lived only for the day.

Berenice – I call out her name – Berenice! And a thousand sweet voices answer me from the past. I can see her clearly now, as she was in her early days of beauty and light. I see her . . . and then suddenly all is darkness, mystery and fear.

Her bright young days ended when an illness – a terrible illness – came down on her like a sudden storm. I watched the dark cloud pass over her. I saw it change her body and mind completely. The cloud came and went, leaving someone I did not know. Who was this sad person I saw now? Where was my Berenice, the Berenice I once knew?

This first illness caused several other illnesses to follow. One of these was a very unusual type of epilepsy.* This epilepsy always came suddenly, without warning. Suddenly, her mind stopped working. She fell to the ground, red in the face, shaking all over, making strange sounds, her eyes not seeing any more. The epilepsy often ended with her going into a kind of very deep sleep. Sometimes, this sleep was so deep that it was difficult to tell if she was dead or not. Often she woke up from the sleep as

* *Epilepsy.* A serious illness in which, for a short time, the mind stops working, everything goes black, and the body jumps and shakes.

suddenly as the epilepsy began. She would just get up again as if nothing was wrong.

It was during this time that *my* illness began to get worse. I felt it growing stronger day by day. I knew I could do nothing to stop it. And soon, like Berenice, my illness changed my life completely.

It was not my body that was sick; it was my mind. It was an illness of the mind. I can only describe it as a type of monomania.* I often lost myself for hours, deep in thought about something – something so unimportant that it seemed funny afterwards. But I am afraid it may be impossible to describe how fully I could lose myself in the useless study of even the simplest or most ordinary object.

I could sit for hours looking at one letter of a word on a page. I could stay, for most of a summer's day, watching a shadow on the floor. I could sit without taking my eyes off a wood fire in winter, until it burnt away to nothing. I could sit for a whole night dreaming about the sweet smell of a flower. I often repeated a single word again and again for hours until the sound of it had no more meaning for me. When I did these things, I always lost all idea of myself, all idea of time, of movement, even of being alive.

There must be no mistake. You must understand that this monomania was not a kind of dreaming. Dreaming is completely different. The dreamer –I am talking about the dreamer who is awake, not asleep – needs and uses the mind to build his dream. Also, the dreamer nearly always *forgets* the thought or idea or object that began his dream. But with me, the object that began the journey into deepest thought always stayed in my mind. The object was always there at the centre of my

* *Monomania.* Thinking about one thing, or idea, and not being able to stop.

thinking. It was the centre of *everything*. It was both the *subject* and the *object* of my thoughts. My thoughts always, always came back to that object in a never-ending circle. The object was no longer real, but still I could not pull myself away from it!

I never loved Berenice, even during the brightest days of her beauty. This is because I have *never* had feelings of the heart. My loves have always been in the world of the mind.

In the grey light of early morning, among the dancing shadows of the forest, in the silence of my library at night, Berenice moved quickly and lightly before my eyes. I never saw my Berenice as a living Berenice. For me, Berenice was a Berenice in a dream. She was not a person of this world – no, I never thought of her as someone real. Berenice was the *idea* of Berenice. She was something to think about, not someone to love.

And so why did I feel differently after her illness? Why, when she was so terribly and sadly changed, did I shake and go white when she came near me?

Because I saw the terrible waste of that sweet and loving person. Because now there was nothing left of the Berenice I once knew!

It is true I never loved her. But I knew she always loved me – deeply. And so, one day – *because I felt so sorry for her* – I had a stupid and evil idea. I asked her to marry me.

Our wedding day was growing closer, and one warm afternoon I was sitting in the library. The clouds were low and dark, the air was heavy, everything was quiet. Suddenly, lifting my eyes from my book, I saw Berenice standing in front of me.

She was like a stranger to me, only a weak shadow of the woman I remembered. I could not even remember how

I watched as Berenice's lips made a strange smile that I could not understand. And it was then that I saw the teeth.

she was before. God, she was so thin! I could see her arms and legs through the grey clothes that hung round her wasted body.

She said nothing. And I could not speak. I do not know why, but suddenly I felt a terrible fear pressing down like a great stone on my heart. I sat there in my chair, too afraid to move.

Her long hair fell around her face. She was as white as snow. She looked strangely calm and happy. But there was no life at all in her eyes. They did not even seem to see me. I watched as her thin, bloodless lips slowly opened. They made a strange smile that I could not understand. And it was then that I saw *the teeth.*

Oh, why did she have to smile at me! Why did I have to see those teeth?

♦

I heard a door closing and I looked up. Berenice was not there any more. The room was empty. But *her teeth* did not leave the room of my mind! I now saw them more clearly than when she was standing in front of me. Every smallest part of each tooth was burnt into my mind. *The teeth*! There they were in front of my eyes – here, there, everywhere I looked. And they were so *white*, with her bloodless lips always moving round them!

I tried to fight this sudden, terrible monomania, but it was useless. All I could think about, all I could see in my mind's eye was the teeth. They were now the centre of my life. I held them up in my mind's eye, looked at them in every light, turned them every way. I studied their shapes, their differences; and the more I thought about them, the more I began to want them. Yes, I *wanted* them! I had to have the teeth! Only *the teeth* could bring me happiness, could stop me from going mad.

Evening came; then darkness turned into another day; soon a second night was falling, and I sat there alone, never moving. I was still lost in thought, in that one same thought: *the teeth*. I saw them everywhere I looked – in the evening shadows, in the darkness in front of my eyes.

Then a terrible cry of horror woke me from my dreams. I heard voices, and more cries of sadness and pain. I got up and opened the door of the library. A servant girl was standing outside, crying.

'Your cousin, sir' she began. 'It was her epilepsy, sir. She died this morning.'

This morning? I looked out of the window. Night was falling . . .

'We are ready to bury her now,' said the girl.

♦

I found myself waking up alone in the library again. I thought that I could remember unpleasant and excited dreams, but I did not know what they were. It was midnight.

'They buried Berenice soon after dark,' I told myself again and again. But I could only half-remember the hours since then – hours full of a terrible unknown horror.

I knew something happened during the night, but I could not remember what it was: those hours of the night were like a page of strange writing that I could not understand.

Next, I heard the high cutting scream of a woman. I remember thinking: 'What did I do? I asked myself this question out loud. And the walls of the library answered me in a soft voice like mine: *What did you do?*

There was a lamp on the table near me, with a small box next to it. I knew this box well – it belonged to our family's doctor. But why was it there, now, on the table? And why was I shaking like a leaf as I looked at it? Why was my hair standing on my head?

There was a knock on the door. A servant came in. He was wild with fear and spoke to me quickly, in a low, shaking voice. I could not understand all of what he was saying.

'Some of us heard a wild cry during the night, sir' he said. 'We went to find out what it was, and we found Berenice's body lying in the open, sir!' he cried. 'Someone took her out of the hole where we buried her! Her body was cut and bleeding! But worse than that, she . . . *she was not dead, sir! She was still alive!*'

25

Dentist's tools fell out of the box, and with them — so small and so white! — thirty-two teeth fell here, there, everywhere.

He pointed at my clothes. There was blood all over them. I said nothing.

He took my hand. I saw cuts and dried blood on it. I cried out, jumped to the table and tried to open the box. I tried and tried but I could not! It fell to the floor and broke. Dentist's tools fell out of it, and with them – so small and so white! – thirty-two teeth fell here, there, everywhere . . .

The Prince locked the great door of the house and threw the key over the wall, into the lake outside.

The Mask of the Red Death

For a long time the Red Death was everywhere in the land. There never was a plague* that killed as many, and there never was a death as terrible.

First, you felt burning pains in your stomach. Then everything began to turn round and round inside your head. Then blood began to come out through your skin – yes, you began to bleed all over your body – but most of all through your face.

And of course when people saw this they left you immediately. Nobody wanted to help you – your horrible red face told everyone that it was too late. Yes, the Red Death was a very short 'illness' – only about half an hour, from its beginning to your end.

But Prince Prospero was a brave and happy and wise prince. When half of the people in his land were dead, he chose a thousand healthy and happy friends and took them away from the city. He took them over the hills and far away, to his favourite house, in the middle of a forest.

It was a very large and beautiful house, with a high, strong wall all round it. The wall had only one door: a very strong metal one. When the Prince and all his friends were safely inside, several servants pushed the great door shut. Looking pleased with himself, the Prince locked it and threw the key (it was the only one) over the wall into the lake outside. He smiled as he watched the circles in the deep dark water. Now nobody could come in or out of the house. Inside, there was plenty of food, enough for more than a year. He and his lucky friends did not have to worry

* *Plague*. A serious illness that goes from person to person very quickly, killing nearly everyone.

about the 'Red Death' outside. The outside world could worry about itself!

And so everyone soon forgot the terrible plague. They were safe inside the Prince's beautiful house, and they had everything they needed to have a good time. There were dancers, there were musicians, there was Beauty, there was wine. All this (and more) was inside. The Red Death was outside.

Five months later — the plague was still everywhere in the land — Prince Prospero gave a very special party for his thousand friends. It was a masked party of a most unusual kind.

Prince Prospero gave this party in the newest part of his great house, in seven rooms which he almost never used. Normally, only the most important visitors used those rooms, foreign princes, for example. They were very unusual, those seven rooms, and that is why he chose them for the party. Prince Prospero often had very unusual ideas. He was a very unusual — a very *strange* — person.

First of all, the rooms were not in a straight line. Walking through them, you came to a turn every twenty or thirty yards. So you could only ever see into one other room at a time. Yes, it was a strange part of the house, and in every room the furniture was different. With each turn you always saw something interesting and new.

In every room there were two tall and narrow windows, one on either side. There was coloured glass in these windows, a different colour in each room. This — and everything else, of course — was the Prince's idea (I forgot to tell you: the Prince made the plans for this part of the house himself).

Of course it was the Prince who decorated the rooms for the party, and he did this in his usual unusual way. Like the glass, each room was a different colour. And everything in each room was that same colour. The first room, at the east end, was blue, and so were the windows: bright blue. In the second room everything was purple, like the glass. In the third everything was green. The fourth was orange, the fifth white, the sixth yellow. In the seventh room everything was black — everything but the windows. They were a deep, rich, red colour, the colour of blood.

There were no lamps anywhere in the seven rooms. Light came from the windows on either side. Outside each window there was a fire burning in a large metal dish. These fires filled the rooms with bright, rich and strangely beautiful colours. But in the west room — the black room — the blood-coloured light was *horrible*. It gave a terrible, wild look to the faces of those who went in. Few people were brave enough to put one foot inside.

A very large clock stood against the far wall of the black room. The great machine made a low, heavy *clang . . . clang . . . clang . . .* sound. Once every hour, when the minute-hand came up to twelve, it made a sound that was so loud, so deep, so clear, and so . . . *richly*, so *strangely* musical that the musicians stopped playing to listen to it. All the dancers stopped dancing. The whole party stopped. Everybody listened to the sound . . . And as they listened, some people's faces became white . . . Other people's heads began to go *round and round* . . . Others put hands to their heads, surprised by sudden strange, *dream-like* thoughts . . . And when the sound died away, there was a strange silence. Light laughs began to break the silence. People laughed quietly, quickly. The musicians looked at each other and smiled. They promised that when the next hour came they would not be so stupid. They would not stop and listen like that. They would go on playing, without listening at all.

But then, three thousand six hundred seconds later, the clock made the same sound again. And again, everything stopped. Again the people's faces became white; again those strange, dream-like thoughts went through people's minds; and again there was that same empty silence, those same quiet laughs, and those same smiles and promises.

31

But, if we forget this, it was a wonderful party. Yes, we can say that the Prince had a truly fine eye for colour! And all his friends enjoyed his strange decorations. Some people thought he was mad, of course (only friends who knew him well knew he was not).

But he did more than choose the decorations. He also chose the way everyone was dressed. Oh yes, you can be sure that they were dressed strangely! And many of them were much more than just strange. Yes, there was a bit of everything at that party: the beautiful, the ugly, and a lot of the horrible. They looked like a madman's dreams, those strange masked people, dancing to the wild music. They went up and down, changing colour as they danced from room to room ... until the minute-hand on the clock came up to the hour ... And then, when they heard the first sound of the clock, everything stopped as before.

The dreams stood still until the great deep voice of the clock died away. Then there was that same strange silence. Then there were those little light and quiet laughs. Then the music began again. The dreams began to move once more, dancing more happily than ever. They danced and danced, on and on, through all the rooms except one. No one went into the west room any more. The blood-coloured light was growing brighter and more horrible with every minute.

But in other rooms the party was going stronger than ever. The wild dancing went on and on until the minute-hand reached that hour again. Then, of course, when the first sound of the clock was heard, the music stopped, the dancers became still, all was still.

It was midnight. One, two, three, four, five ... Twelve times, the clock made that same, strange, deep and so *sweetly* musical sound. Midnight ... seven, eight ... It seemed like there was no end to the sounds this time. Each sound seemed to go on for

The stranger was wearing black clothes. His mask was the face of a dead man – the mask of the Red Death.

ever. And as those twelve sounds went on and on and on... people became whiter... Their heads began to go round and round and round... They thought stranger and more dream-like thoughts than ever before... And some of them saw a tall masked man walking slowly and silently among them.

The news travelled quickly through the rooms. Soon, everybody at the party was talking about the tall masked man. As the stranger walked silently among them, people looked at him with anger, and horror. Anger at choosing those clothes! *Horror* at choosing that mask! If it was to make them laugh, then it was not funny! Even the *Prince* would never dream of wearing those clothes.

The stranger was wearing black clothes. His mask was the face of a dead man. Yes, it was a death mask, but it was the *colour* of that mask that made everyone shake with horror. The mask was red. It was the mask of the Red Death.

Prince Prospero saw the stranger as he walked among the dancers, and suddenly he became mad with anger. He waved his hand and the music stopped immediately.

'Who?' he shouted, 'Who has done this horrible thing! Catch that man! Take off that mask! We will cut off his head in the morning!'

The masked stranger began walking slowly towards the Prince as he said this. Everybody – even the brave Prince Prospero – was suddenly afraid. Nobody was brave enough to put out a hand to stop the visitor. He passed very close to the Prince, and everybody, everywhere, stepped back against the walls as he walked slowly out of the blue room and into the purple, through the green into the orange, into the white, into the yellow...

Suddenly, Prince Prospero was angry with himself for being so stupidly afraid. He ran after the stranger. He ran through the six rooms – but nobody followed him.

Pulling out his knife, he ran into the black room. The masked man, who was walking towards the opposite corner, stopped. The Prince stopped, a yard from him. The masked man turned suddenly, and a terrible, cutting cry was heard. The Prince's shining knife fell without a sound on the black floor. The Prince fell without a sound next to it. Dead.

Suddenly – and nobody knew why – suddenly, the dancers were no longer afraid. A crowd of them ran into the black room. They ran to the stranger who was standing in the shadow of the great clock. When they caught him, the mask and the empty clothes fell to the floor. Everyone cried out in horror. There was nobody inside the clothes! There was nobody there. The man's body was nothing but air.

Everyone understood that the Red Death was now among them. He came like a thief in the night. And as the seconds

The empty clothes fell to the floor. There was nobody there.
The man's body was nothing but air.

passed – clang . . . clang . . . clang . . . – one by one, people began to die the terrible death. Soon, everywhere, the floors of the seven rooms were wet with blood.

When the last person died, the last lamp went out. And when that last lamp went out, the life of the clock stopped with it.

And everything was silence and darkness.

ACTIVITIES

The Black Cat

Before you read

1 Look at the Word List at the back of the book. Find any new words in your dictionary. Then find:
   a two words for people
   b two feelings
   c one thing that shows a face and one thing that hides a face
   d a thing for cutting and a thing for lighting a dark room

2 Read the Introduction to this book and answer these questions.
   a Who kills what in 'The Black Cat'?
   b Whose face is in the portrait in 'The Oval Portrait'?
   c What is the stranger wearing in 'The Mask of the Red Death'?
   d What did Poe write stories about?
   e Which part of his life was happy?

3 Look at the pictures in the first story. Do you think the man has a happy life? Why (not)?

While you read

4 Put these sentences in the correct order. Write 1–8. The person who tells the story:
   a cuts out one of Pluto's eyes with a knife.   .....
   b begins drinking too much and becomes more selfish.   .....
   c hangs his cat from a tree until it is dead.   .....
   d sees the shape of a cat hanging by its neck in the
      wet plaster.   .....
   e finds a black cat that follows him home.   .....
   f marries a woman who also loves animals.   .....
   g escapes with his wife from their burning house.   .....
   h begins hitting his wife and hurting his dear Pluto.   .....

5 Are these sentences about the second cat right (✓) or wrong (✗)?
The second cat:
   a has two green eyes.   .....
   b frightens the story-teller until he feels horror.   .....
   c has a white shape of the gallows on his chest.   .....
   d wakes the story-teller nearly every hour in the night.   .....
   e is killed with an axe and is hidden in a wall in the cellar.   .....
   f disappears after the murder, making the story-teller free.   .....
   g screams from inside the cellar wall so that the police
       discover the story-teller's crime.   .....

After you read
6 Discuss with another student. Why does the story-teller say these
sentences?
   a 'Yes, this story ends with *my* end, with my death tomorrow.'
   b 'I have always loved animals more than anything.'
   c 'It was that evil enemy of Man called *Drink* . . .'
   d 'There was not the smallest piece of good left in me.'
   e 'Yes, this is a well-built old house, isn't it?'
7 Why are these important to the story?
   a Drink
   b wet plaster
   c an axe
   d gallows

The Oval Portrait

Before you read
8 Look at the picture on page 12. Where are the men on horses
going? Look at the pictures on pages 15 and 17. What do you
see?
9 Why do some people decorate their houses with portraits of the
people in their family? Would you like to sit for a portrait? Why
(not)?

10 Circle the best word in *italics*.

  a The servant lights the *fire / lamp* next to his employer's bed.

  b The eyes of the woman in the portrait fill the story-teller with surprise at first, but later with *happiness / horror*.

  c The painter loves his *wife / work* more than anything in the world.

  d The painter's wife hates his paintings because they take all of his *time / money*.

  e The painter's wife is becoming *famous / unhealthy*, but he never notices.

  f Nearly completed, the portrait makes the painter almost *mad / romantic*.

  g Looking at his finished portrait of his wife, he thinks she looks *dead / alive*.

  h The painter's wife *sleeps / dies* while her husband paints her portrait.

After you read

11 At the following times, how has the painter's wife changed?

  a soon after their marriage

  b when visitors speak about the portrait

  c when the portrait is finished

12 What feelings do these people have?

  a The story-teller for the oval portrait

  b The young wife for her husband

  c The painter for his wife

  d The painter for his portrait of his wife

Berenice

Before you read

13 Look at the picture on page 18. Where do you think the man is? Does he look happy or sad, rich or poor?

14 Look at the picture on page 23. What is the man looking at? What does he knock on to the floor in the picture on page 26?

15 Finish sentences a–e. Write 1–5.

    a Egaeus's favourite room is ...   .

    b Because Egaeus almost never leaves the house, ...

    c Egaeus's cousin Berenice is completely different but ...   .

    d Sometimes people cannot be sure that ...   .

    e Egaeus becomes ill in his mind. He loses ...   .

    1) the library, where he was born and his mother died.

    2) her bright young days end with the start of epilepsy.

    3) she is alive.

    4) the wild ideas inside his head are his real world.

    5) himself in the useless study of ordinary objects.

16 Write the missing word from the story.

    a Egaeus loses all idea of himself and all idea of time because he suffers from ....

    b For Egaeus, Berenice is not a real person of this world; she is a woman in a ....

    c Egaeus has never loved Berenice but he feels sorry for her. So he asks her to .... him.

    d After Berenice smiles at Egaeus, he can not get her .... out of his mind.

    e A .... girl tells him that Berenice is dead.

    f Something happened in the night after they .... Berenice.

    g Berenice is badly cut, and Egaeus has .... on his clothes.

After you read

17 Choose the best way to complete the sentences.

    a When he tells this story, Egaeus is ... .

      a young man   in the middle of his life   married

    b As a girl, Berenice is happy, healthy, beautiful and ... .

      thinks a lot   lives in the library   often goes out

    c After Egaeus becomes ill, he often cannot stop thinking about one ... .

      object   person   book

    d Berenice ... Egaeus.

       loves   feels sorry for   doesn't want to marry

    e Berenice is buried but ... .

       without her teeth   she is not dead   Egaeus does not know.

    f Berenice wakes up ... .

       under the ground   in the library   without any teeth

18 Explain what Egaeus means when he says:

    a And soon, like Berenice, my illness changed my life completely.

    b She was like a stranger to me, only a weak shadow of the woman I remembered.

    c Oh, why did she have to smile at me!

    d Only *the teeth* could bring me happiness, could stop me from going mad.

19 Why are these important to Egaeus?

    a the library

    b Berenice's health and illness

    c the doctor's box

The Mask of the Red Death

Before you read

20 Look at the picture on page 28. What is the man doing? Why is he doing that, do you think?

21 Look at the picture on page 33. What are the people wearing? How do they feel about the man in front of them?

22 What is happening in the picture on page 35, do you think? Why?

While you read

23 Put a (✓) next to the best way to finish these sentences.

    a When people get the Red Death, first they feel pains in their stomachs. Then in their heads they

       • have a terrible headache.   .....

       • imagine strange thoughts.   .....

       • feel everything turning round and round.   .....

b The Red Death makes people's faces
- red hot. .....
- bloody. .....
- a strange grey colour. .....

c Prince Prospero takes a thousand healthy friends to his house far away. He throws away the only key so that
- nobody can come in or out of the house. .....
- his friends will worry about their future. .....
- he can keep his friends there for ever. .....

d The Prince gives a masked party in seven rooms which are
- in a straight line so you can see into each room. .....
- each decorated in a different colour. .....
- without windows. .....

e The seventh room, the black room, is different from the others because the windows are
- tall and narrow. .....
- painted with blood. .....
- not the same colour as the room. .....

24 Write 'Yes' or 'No' after each question.

a Does the fire outside the black room fill the room with a beautiful red light? ....

b When the clock makes a low, heavy sound, do the musicians, dancers and guests feel strange? ....

c Do some people think that the Prince is mad? ....

d Do the guests laugh when they see the tall masked man in his black clothes and mask? ....

e Does the Prince kill the tall masked man with his knife in the black room? ....

After you read

25 How do the guests feel when:

a Prince Prospero takes them to his house in the forest? Why?

b the clock makes its low, heavy sound every hour? Why?

c the dancers run into the black room and catch the stranger? Why?

26 Discuss these questions. What do you think?

    a Why does Prince Prospero make the newest part of his house so strange?

    b Is he a good Prince or a bad Prince? Why?

    c What did Poe want people to learn from this story?

27 Work with another student. You are guests at the party. The clock has just made its strange sound for the second time. Have this conversation.

    Student A: Describe the strange feelings that you had. You feel worried now. Ask how your friend feels.

    Student B: You are surprised by the strange dream-like thoughts you had. But now you think it was funny. Try to calm your friend's fears.

Writing

28 In 'The Black Cat' the police find the dead woman after they hear the cat's screams. Write about this for the local newspaper.

29 Imagine you are the brother or sister of the story-teller in 'The Black Cat'. You want to save your brother from the gallows. You believe that he is not evil; he needs help. Write a letter. Explain why he should go to a special hospital.

30 Imagine you are the story-teller in 'The Oval Portrait'. You have sat up all night looking at the portrait and reading about the beautiful young woman. Write about your feelings for the young woman and your opinion of her portrait.

31 Write about Poe's opinion of the painter in 'The Oval Portrait'. Think about the language he uses when he describes the painter and his wife's feelings for his work.

32 What do you think happens to Egaeus in 'Berenice' after the teeth fall out of the box and onto the floor? Write an ending for this story.

33 Imagine you are Berenice at the end of the story. Write a description of Egaeus. Write about your feelings for him and his for you. What kind of man is he? Why did he pull out your teeth, do you think?

34 Imagine you are one of the Prince's guests in 'The Mask of the Red Death'. It is the night before the masked party. A friend of yours is still in the city and is still alive. Write a letter to him asking about his family. Tell him about the Prince's house and your life inside it.

35 Imagine it is many years after the plague ended. You find Prince Prospero's house in the forest and climb inside. Write about what you find there. Write your opinion of what happened.

36 Which of these stories is the best, do you think? Why? Write your answer.

37 Choose one story. Explain how Poe uses illness, madness and fear to produce a feeling of horror.

WORD LIST

among (prep) in a group of

anger (n) the feeling of being angry

axe (n) a sharp tool for cutting wood

beauty (n) what makes things beautiful

bury (v) to put a dead body under the ground

cellar (n) a room under a house

decorate (v) to add things to something to make it look nicer

evil (adj) very bad and hurting people badly

horror (n) a very strong feeling of fear of something very bad and ugly

lamp (n) a thing that produces light

lips (n) the redder or darker parts of skin around your mouth

mad (adj) ill in the mind

mask (n/v) something that a person wears to hide or protect the face

object (n) a thing that you can see, hold or touch

oval (adj) a shape like a circle but longer than it is wide

plaster (n) the covering on walls that makes them smooth

portrait (n) a picture of a person

servant (n) somebody who works for a person or family in their home

several (quant) more than a few

stranger (n) a person who you do not know